A GUIDE TO NIGHT SOUNDS

A GUIDE TO NIGHT SOUNDS

Lang Elliott

NatureSound Studio

STACKPOLE BOOKS

Published by
STACKPOLE BOOKS
5067 Ritter Road
Mechanicsburg, PA 17055
www.stackpolebooks.com

Printed in China

10 9 8 7 6 5 4 3 2 1

This is a revised and expanded edition of the book originally published in 1992 by NatureSound Studio and in 1994 by NorthWord Press.

Cover design by Wendy A. Reynolds

Pencil drawings by Cynthia J. Page

Photo credits: Ron Austing: cover, 16, 20; Lang Elliott: 2, 8, 22, 25, 26, 40, 42, 44–45, 46, 48, 50–51; Todd Fink/Daybreak Imagery: 4; Richard Day/Daybreak Imagery: 10–11, 14, 28, 32, 36; Gerry Lemmo: 52, 56–57

Library of Congress Cataloging-in-Publication Data

Elliott, Lang.
  A guide to night sounds / Lang Elliott.
     p. cm.
  "This is a revised and expanded edition of the book originally published in 1994 by Northword Press"—T.p. verso.
  ISBN 0-8117-3164-2
  1. Birdsongs—Identification. 2. Animal sounds—Identification. 3. Nocturnal birds—Identification. 4. Nocturnal animals—Identification. I. Title.
QL698.5.E4523 2004
591.59'4—dc22
                                                          2004003971

Contents

Credits and Acknowledgments

A *Guide to Night Sounds* was created, narrated, and produced by Lang Elliott, owner and operator of NatureSound Studio.

The Sound Recordings: The majority of recordings used in this work were collected in the field by Lang Elliott. Additional recordings were supplied by Bill Evans, Geoff Keller, and Ted Mack.

We at NatureSound Studio offer our deepest thanks to the abundance of wild creatures that made this production possible: the native birds, frogs, mammals, insects, and reptiles that grace the nighttime landscape with their incredible sounds. May they continue to thrive for eons to come!

*O*f all the sounds of nature, the magical voices of the night fascinate us beyond compare. Who has not been moved by the distant hoots of owls, the incessant croaks of frogs, the deafening trills of insects, or the sudden snorts, howls, grunts, and whines made by mammals and other denizens of the night?

Much of our fascination stems from the fact that night-active animals are not easily seen. We are excited by their incredible sounds, but only with difficulty can we identify the sound makers. When mysterious sounds spring forth unexpectedly from the darkness, our imaginations run wild. Unidentified creature-sounds transform into ghostly utterances, and soon our hearts are pounding in fearful anticipation.

With the help of this audio guide, you will learn to recognize and identify an amazing assortment of night sounds. Your appreciation will increase as you learn the delightful stories behind the sounds and acquire the ability to associate images with the sounds themselves. As your knowledge expands your excitement will grow, and your night sound experience will soon become richer than you ever imagined.

Follow me . . . on this fantastic journey into the night!

Green Frog

I. Thrushes

Veery

*T*he Thrush family (Turdidae), which includes the familiar robin and the bluebirds, contains some of the finest musicians in the songbird group. The Veery and several species that bear the name "thrush" are slightly smaller than robins (about 7 inches long) and have brownish backs and spotted breasts. All have exquisite, flutelike songs that are often sung at dusk, just before the thrushes go to roost for the night.

Twilight song of the Hermit Thrush

Wood Thrush: A common woodland species that ranges throughout most of the East. The song begins with soft (and sometimes inaudible) *tut* notes, followed by variable flutelike phrases that sound like *eee-o-lay-o-leee* or *eee-o-leee*.

Veery: Breeds in the Northeast, southern Canada, and in the western mountain states. Prefers moist woodlands. Named for its unforgettable, ethereal song, which sounds like a hollow, downward spiraling *veera-veera-veera-veera*.

Hermit Thrush: Found in conifer forests in the Northeast, through much of Canada, and in most of the western states. Song begins with a clear, whistled note, followed by a jumble of flutelike phrases.

Swainson's Thrush: Prefers moist woodlands in the Northeast, Canada, and the western states. Breezy, flutelike song consists of a series of musical phrases that seem to spiral upward in pitch.

Chuck-will's-widow

The nightjars are drab-colored night hunters that capture flying insects by snaring them with their wide, gaping mouths. Nightjars roost on the ground by day, camouflaged by their mottled plumage. Males sing at night from perches on or near the ground. The name "nightjar" derives from the jarring night sounds made by a European species. Nightjars are also referred to as "goatsuckers" due to an old folk legend that they suckle milk from goats at night.

Whip-poor-will: 10 inches long. Fairly common in eastern woodlands, but absent from the extreme South. Male's song is a loud, whistled *whip-poor-will, whip-poor-will, whip-poor-will* repeated for long periods. A soft introductory note may be heard at close distances.

Whip-poor-will perched on a log

*Nighthawks **peenting** overhead*

Chuck-will's-widow: Our largest nightjar (12 inches long). Breeds in pine forests of the Southeast. Male's song is easily confused with that of the whip-poor-will, but has a different cadence and is accented on the second and third syllables: *chuck-WILL'S-WID-ow, chuck-WILL'S-WID-ow* . . .

Common Poorwill: Our smallest nightjar (less than 8 inches long). Ranges throughout much of the West; prefers sagebrush and chaparral habitats. Distant song sounds like a melancholy *poor-will* repeated time and again. At close range, a terminal *ip* note can be heard: *poor-will-ip, poor-will-ip, poor-will-ip* . . .

Common Nighthawk: About 10 inches long. Found throughout most of North America. Day-active as well as night-active. Unlike other nightjars, the nighthawk has pointed wings with white wing bars, and darts about in the air with sudden, erratic motions. The nighthawk's flight call is a loud, nasal *peent!* The courtship display of the male, performed at dusk, dawn, or at night, is unique: he dives toward the ground and then swoops upward at the last moment, making a hollow, booming *phhrrrt!* or *phooooph!* with the stiff feathers of his wings.

Common Snipe

*T*he shorebirds are a diverse group of small to medium-size birds known for their habit of feeding along sandy or muddy shorelines. Included in this group are plovers, sandpipers, dowitchers, stilts, willets, curlews, avocets, sanderlings, and a variety of other species. Most are day-active, but some may be heard at night.

American Woodcock: An odd-looking, nocturnal species (11 inches long) with a short neck, short legs, long beak, and a chunky overall appearance. Found in the East; prefers wet forests and thickets. Woodcocks have

A strutting Woodcock **peents**

Killdeer

Snipe winnowing over marsh at night

long, fleshy beaks that they use to probe for earthworms in moist earth at night. During the spring breeding season, courting males fly to open areas at dusk. Each male struts about on the ground, making buzzy, nasal *peent* calls. The courting male then takes flight, rising above his territory in a spiraling ascent, all the while making a high-pitched twitter with the help of special feathers on his wings. At the apex of his flight, a hundred or more feet above the ground, the male drops from the sky and plummets with a zig-zag motion, making whimpering whistles as he falls. Returning to the ground, he *peent*s and struts for awhile and then repeats his amazing aerial display.

Common Snipe: A stocky, short-legged marsh dweller (11 inches long). Resembles the woodcock, but is not as chunky. Found throughout Canada, in the northern states, and over much of the West. Males court in spring and early summer, often at night, by flying in wide circles above their territories, dipping downward periodically and spreading their tail feathers to produce an eerie winnowing *hoo-hoo-hoo-hoo-hoo-hoo*.

Killdeer: Widely distributed; perhaps the best known of all our native shorebirds (10 inches long). Recognized by its two black breast bands. Frequents shorelines, but often nests and feeds on ground in dry, barren areas far from water. Named for its plaintive, piercing calls, which are often heard at night: *ki-dee, ki-deah,* or *ki-dee-dee*.

Black-necked Stilt: A sleek and graceful wader about 14 inches long. Black above and white below with spindly, stilt-like legs that approach 10 inches in length. Stilts breed in western marshlands and, more rarely, in wetlands along the Atlantic and Gulf coasts. Primary call is a sharp, repeated *kip, kip, kip, kip,* often given in flight.

Black-necked Stilt

4. Ducks and Geese

Canada Goose

*T*he ducks and geese, along with swans, are collectively known as waterfowl because they feed and breed in lakes, ponds, and streams. About 43 species inhabit North America. Most are primarily day-active, but some species migrate at night and vocalize while flying. Ducks and geese also sound off when disturbed at nighttime roosts.

Mallard: Our best-known and perhaps most abundant native duck (24 inches long). Drake (male) recognized by metallic green head, yellow bill, narrow white collar, and chestnut breast. Hen is mottled brown. Mallards rest quietly in marshy areas at night. When frightened, hens quack loudly as they burst from the surface of the water.

Canada Goose: Our most common and familiar goose (up to 48 inches long). Breeds from the arctic and subarctic southward into the northern half of the United States. Migrates in V-formation by day or night. Primary call is a deep, musical *ah-honk*, often given in flight.

Mallard bursting into flight

5. Owls

Barn Owl in flight

*O*f all the night-active birds, owls excite us like no others. There are 19 species in North America. Most hunt at night and rest by day. All have large eyes and heads, keen hearing, sharp talons, and fringed wing feathers that allow for silent flight. Owls are an incredibly vocal group. They hoot, screech, whistle, trill, and make a variety of other interesting calls.

Barred Owl: A chunky, dark-brown owl with streaked belly and round head. About 20 inches long. Primarily eastern, but expanding range into the Northwest. Inhabits a variety of forest habitats. Especially fond of wooded swamps in the South and Southeast. Distinctive hoot-series sounds like: *Who cooks for you . . . Who cooks for you all?* Members of a pair or family group often participate in lively vocal exchanges comprised of *hoot*s, *haw*s, and *hoo-aw*s. Young make harsh screeches and other odd sounds.

Barred Owl

Great Horned Owl:
A large owl (up to 25 inches long) with prominent earlike tufts of feathers ("ear tufts") on its head. May take prey as large as chickens, skunks, or porcupines. Primary call is a series of five or six low, resonant hoots: *hooo, hahoo, hooo, hooo.* Female is larger than male but has a higher-pitched hoot. Young utter harsh, whistling screams that are thought to be hunger cries.

Great Horned Owl

Eastern Screech-Owl:
A small owl (9 inches long) with prominent ear tufts. Two color phases: one reddish-brown and the other gray. Common in a variety of habitats throughout most of eastern United States, including suburban woodlots. Prominent call is an eerie, wavering whistle (the "whinny call") that

Eastern Screech-Owl

Barn Owl

descends in pitch. Also makes a soft, extended trill (the "monotonic trill" or "bounce call").

Western Screech-Owl: Almost identical in appearance to gray-phase Eastern Screech-Owl. About 9 inches long. Common in a variety of habitats, including suburban settings. Primary call is a series of tooting whistles that accelerate in tempo.

Barn Owl: A pale-colored owl, whitish below, rusty above, and with a white, heart-shaped face. About 16 inches long and lacking ear tufts. Widespread throughout most of the United States, but most common in the West. Prefers open country. Nests in old silos, barn lofts, and dark places in old buildings, sometimes in city settings. Common call is a loud, raspy, hissing screech: *SKEEEESCH!*

Red and gray Eastern Screech-Owls

Northern Saw-whet Owl

Northern Saw-whet Owl: A small owl that lacks ear tufts. Only 7 to 8 inches long, smaller than screech-owls. Adults reddish-brown above and white below with reddish streaks on breast. Prefers dense evergreens and mixed woods. Difficult to locate but tame when approached. Breeding call is a monotonous series of tooting whistles that are repeated mechanically for long periods.

6. Frogs and Toads

Green Frog

About 95 species of frogs and toads are found in the United States and Canada. They range in size from about 1 inch long (Cricket Frogs) to nearly 8 inches long (Bullfrogs). The males of most species produce mating calls during the breeding season. Throat pouches called vocal sacs are inflated when calling; these provide added resonance. The mating calls of most species are distinctive and allow for positive identification of the species.

Spring Peeper: About 1 inch long; brownish color. Has sticky toe-pads. One of the most abundant eastern frogs. Breeds in pools, ponds, and lakes. Male's call is a high, piping whistle or peep.

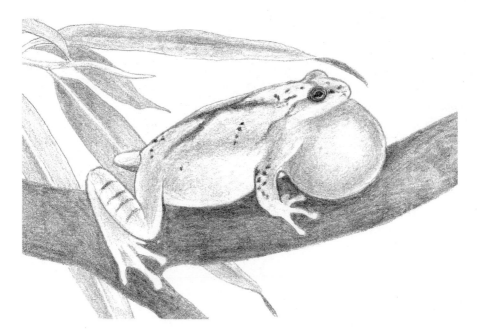

Spring Peeper

Pacific Treefrog: Up to 2 inches long; color varies from green to brown, gray, or black. Abundant in the Pacific Coast region. Male's call is a two-syllable *rib-bit*, repeated about once a second. This species is commonly heard as a background sound in movies made in Hollywood.

Pickerel Frog: Up to 3 inches long; recognized by square spots arranged in two parallel rows on back. Found east of the Great Plains. Male's call is a low-pitched snore of 1 to 2 seconds in duration.

Western Chorus Frog: About 1 inch long; variable color. Common throughout much of the Midwest. Breeds in shallow water. Male's call is a vibrant *crrrreeeek*, a rapid series of metallic clicks that rise in pitch toward the end.

Northern Cricket Frog: About 1 inch long; variable color. Small and warty with dark triangle between eyes. Found through much of the East and Midwest. Breeding call of male is a metallic *gick, gick, gick, gick, gick* that starts slow, then speeds up. Sounds like someone tapping two small stones together.

The Pickerel Frog has paired vocal sacs

Pig Frog

Green Frog: Up to 4 inches long; green to brown. A common frog of pond and lake shorelines in the East. Call is a loud, twanging *goonk* or *tung!* given singly or repeated several times in rapid succession.

Bullfrog: Up to 8 inches long; green to olive brown. Our largest native frog. Abundant in the East; distribution spotty in the West. Found along shorelines of lakes, ponds, and slow-moving streams. Call is low and vibrant: *rum . . . rum . . . jug-o-rum . . . jug-o-rum . . .*

Pig Frog: Up to 5 inches long; green to brown with dark flecks. Common in southeastern swamps and marshes. Call is a deep, piglike grunt, sometimes repeated several times in rapid succession: *unk, unk, unk, unk, unk . . .*

American Toad

American Toad: Up to 5 inches long; brownish and warty. The widespread and abundant "warty toad" of the Northeast and Midwest. Breeds in shallow pools, ditches, and streams. Male's call is a melodic and dreamlike trill lasting up to 30 seconds.

Fowler's Toad and Woodhouse's Toad: 2 to 5 inches long; brownish and warty. The Fowler's Toad ranges throughout much of the East and Midwest. The Woodhouse's Toad is found from the Great Plains to the Southwest. The two species sound almost identical. Breeding call of male is a buzzy, nasal *waaaaah* which lasts from 1 to 3 seconds. Some liken this call to the bleat of a sheep.

Woodhouse's Toad

Clapper Rail

The rails are hen-like marsh birds with secretive habits and unusual voices. Six species inhabit North America. Most prefer thick marsh vegetation and are more often heard than seen. Rails are reluctant fliers and usually run, rather than fly, when frightened. The Common Moorhen is less secretive than the rails and may be seen swimming and wading in marshy areas. Related to the rails and moorhen are the long-necked, long-legged cranes and the Limpkin, a unique subtropical bird found only in swamps and marshes in the extreme Southeast.

Size comparison of Black Rail (left) and Clapper Rail

Clapper Rail: The common "marsh hen" of saltmarsh habitats along the Atlantic, Gulf, and lower Pacific coasts. Gray-brown and about 15 inches long. Loud, clattering call-series sounds like: *kek, kek, kek, kek, kek* . . . Also produces a sudden outburst of grunting *cuk*s. Noisy at dusk, at dawn, and during moonlit nights. The freshwater King Rail hybridizes with the Clapper and produces similar sounds.

Black Rail: Our smallest rail (5 to 6 inches long). Black body with white speckles on back. Very rare and secretive; seldom seen or heard. Prefers grassy or sedgy saltmarsh habitats. Breeding call of male, given at night, is a metallic *ki-ki-kerrrr*, repeated for long periods.

Sora: Common and abundant over much of North America. About 9 inches long; gray-brown with a short, yellow bill. Inhabits dense growth in freshwater and brackish marshes. Often observed feeding along muddy shorelines at marsh edge. The Sora's primary night sound is a plaintive *ker-wee*, given with a rising inflection.

Virginia Rail: About 9 inches long; rusty-brown with a long, slender bill. Common but secretive. Frequents freshwater marshes of the Northeast, the

Virginia Rail running for cover

upper Midwest, and most of the West. Breeding call of the male, often heard at night in the spring, is a metallic ticking: *tic, tic, ki-tic, ki-tic, ki-tic, ki-tic . . .*

Yellow Rail: Small (6 to 7 inches long) and shy. Rarely seen or heard. Yellow-brown in color, with a short bill. Prefers grassy marshes and wet meadows of the upper Midwest and southern Canada. Avoids tall vegetation that other rails seem to like. Breeding call is a long series of sharp clicking notes, given in groups of twos and threes, roughly alternated: *tic-tic, tic-tic-tic, tic-tic, tic-tic-tic*. Easily imitated by tapping two small stones together.

Common Moorhen: Looks ducklike when swimming. About 13 inches long. Dark gray with a red forehead shield and a red bill with a yellow tip. Breeds in freshwater marshes of the East and Southwest. Night-active, it makes a variety of sounds, including a laugh-like outburst of *kuk* calls. Neighboring individuals often respond with similar calls and a wave of "moorhen laughter" spreads across the marsh.

Common Moorhen

Sandhill Cranes in flight

Sandhill Crane: A long-legged and long-necked bird, tall and stately in appearance. Up to 48 inches long with a 6-foot wingspan. Flies with neck extended. Often confused with the Great Blue Heron. Breeds in the upper Midwest and the mountain states, and also in the tundra of the far North. Smaller, non-migratory populations occur in the Southeast. Cranes are wild and wary, nesting and feeding in extensive marshes as well as wet plains or prairies. Primary call, often given at night, is a trumpeting and rattling *ga-rrrroooo*. During the springtime courtship phase, Sandhill Cranes leap into the air with half-spread wings and bow toward one another while making guttural calls.

Limpkin

Limpkin: An exotic-looking, long-necked wader found only in swamps and marshes of Florida. About 26 inches long, chocolate brown with white streaks on upper body. Named for its limping gait. The Limpkin is the lone survivor of an ancient line of birds which goes back 54 million years. Primary call, often given at night, is a loud, wailing scream: *krree-ow, krree-ow, krree-ow* . . . Also referred to as "Night Crier."

8. Alligators and Crocodiles

American Alligator

Alligators and crocodiles are huge, lizard-like reptiles adapted for an aquatic existence in freshwater and saltwater habitats. The American Alligator is our most common native species. The American Crocodile and the Spectacled Caiman (an introduced species) are found only in the extreme southern part of Florida.

American Alligator: Adults can grow to over 15 feet long, but individuals over 10 feet are rare. Recognized by broad, rounded snout and black color (crocodiles have long, tapered snouts and light brown color). Breeds in swamps, bayous, and marshes of the Gulf and lower Atlantic states, including Florida. Lion-like voice of male is a loud, bellowing growl or roar that can be heard at considerable distances.

Great Blue Heron

*T*he Heron family is a diverse group of large wading birds, most having long necks and spear-like bills. Includes the herons, egrets, and bitterns. Members of this group fly with necks folded, unlike the cranes, which fly with necks extended.

Great Blue Heron: The best-known and most widespread of our native herons. Blue-gray in color. Adults have ornate black plumes on head. Our largest North American heron, nearly 50 inches long (4 feet tall) and with a 7-foot wingspan. Active both day and night. When startled, utters low-pitched croaks, given singly or in a short series.

Black-crowned Night-Heron

Black-crowned Night-Heron: A stocky heron with short neck and legs; it is about 25 inches long. Gray-colored, with black cap and back, and white plumes on head. Primarily nocturnal in habits. Frequents freshwater marshes and tidal flats. Call is a low-pitched *wok!*

American Bittern

American Bittern: A stocky wader with brownish, concealing plumage. About 28 inches long. Found in freshwater and saltwater marshes over most of North America. Fairly common but secretive; hides in dense marsh vegetation. Often heard at dusk and sometimes at night. Remarkable breeding call of male is a resonant and pumplike *onk-a-chonk*, repeated several times. Before calling, the male gulps air to inflate his esophagus; this adds resonance to the call. Also referred to as "Thunder Pumper" and "Water Belcher."

Sedge Wren

*T*he wrens are small and energetic songbirds with chunky bodies, slender bills, and uplifted tails. Nine species inhabit North America. Most stay close to the ground as they move about. Wrens are day-active, but two species, the Marsh Wren and Sedge Wren, often sing at night.

Marsh Wren: About 5 inches long; brownish, with white streaks on back and bold white eyeline. Common in freshwater marshes and coastal saltmarshes. Prefers thick vegetation. Males sing exuberantly both day and night while perched with tail cocked upward. Song is a series of loud, gurgling notes, often ending with a rattling trill.

Sedge Wren: About 4 inches long. One of our smallest and most timid wrens. Looks like Marsh Wren, but crown is streaked and white eyeline is not as distinct. Frequents wet grass or sedge meadows. Song is a dry, rattling chatter: *chip, chippy-chap-chap-chap* or *chip, chippy-churrrr*. Males sometime sing at night.

Marsh Wren

White-throated Sparrow

A diverse group of small songbirds, most having short, cone-shaped bills adapted for cracking seeds. As a rule, sparrows are brown and somewhat inconspicuous in appearance. However, the males of many species bring attention to themselves with their colorful songs. Several species regularly sing at night.

White-throated Sparrow: About 7 inches long. Recognized by brown back, gray breast, white throat patch, and yellow spot between eye and bill. Breeds in thickets in coniferous or mixed woods of northeastern United States and Canada. Male's song composed of clear, pure whistles grouped in triplets at the end. Song rhythm usually conforms to the phrase *Old Peabody, Sam Peabody, Peabody, Peabody*. Often sings at night.

12. Mimic Thrushes

Gray Catbird

44

The Mimic Thrushes are a vocal group of thrushlike songbirds. Included in the family are the mockingbirds, catbirds, and thrashers. These birds are referred to as "mimic thrushes" because some mimic the calls of other birds. Catbirds and mockingbirds often sing at night.

Gray Catbird: About 9 inches long; dark gray with black cap and chestnut patch on the underside of the base of the tail. Prefers dense thickets. Common throughout most of the United States and southern Canada, but absent from the Southwest and Pacific Coast. Song is a mixture of melodious and harsh notes grouped in phrases, with each phrase being different from the one that precedes it.

Snowy Tree Cricket

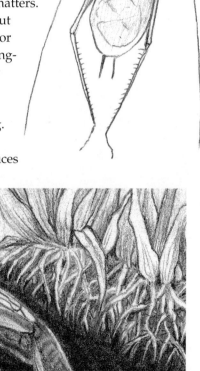

*T*he majority of night-active insect soundmakers belong to the order Orthoptera, which includes the crickets, grasshoppers, and katydids. In these groups, breeding males produce calls with specialized "stridulating" organs located on their wings. These consist of a "file and scraper" mechanism that is used to produce chirps, trills, and grating chatters. Other insect groups also produce sounds, but these may have little to do with breeding. For instance, the bark-eating grubs of certain long-horned beetles produce distinctive chewing sounds as they feed, both day and night.

Snowy Tree Cricket: About $3/4$ inch long. Pale-green cricket with delicate, lacy wings and long antennae. Stridulating male produces

Northern Mole Cricket singing from its burrow entrance

Carolina Ground Cricket

melodic chirps from shrubs, often near the ground. He raises his wings straight up when singing and exposes a gland that secretes a glutinous liquid that the female devours prior to copulation. Often referred to as "temperature cricket" because the number of chirps occurring in 15 seconds plus 40 yields a close approximation of the temperature in Fahrenheit.

Northern Mole Cricket: About 1 inch long. An odd-looking, burrowing cricket with enlarged forelegs adapted for digging. Common throughout most of the East in muddy areas along shorelines or in other wet areas. Male chirps from entrance to his burrow. The song of this species is the lowest-pitched of all our native insect breeding calls.

Carolina Ground Cricket: A member of the subfamily Nemobiinae which includes a variety of different ground crickets. About 1/2 inch long and brownish-black in color. Ranges across most of the United States. Sings from the ground in pastures, lawns, and moist ditches. The song of the male is a high-pitched buzzing trill that often has a pulsating or jerky quality.

Northern True Katydid: About 1 1/2 to 2 inches long; dark green with gauze-like wings and long antennae. Katydids are members of the Long-horned Grasshopper family (Tettigoniidae), named for their long antennae. The Northern True Katydid is common throughout most of the East. Male's harsh call sounds like *ch-ch* or *ch-ch-ch*, given about once every second with rhythm of words *ka-ty* or *ka-ty-did*. Neighboring individuals and large choruses sometimes call in almost perfect unison.

Sword-bearing Cone-headed Grasshopper: Another member of the Long-horned Grasshopper family. About 2 inches long. Slender and green, with long antennae and conical head. Commonly found in tall grass or weeds in the Northeast and upper Midwest, often along

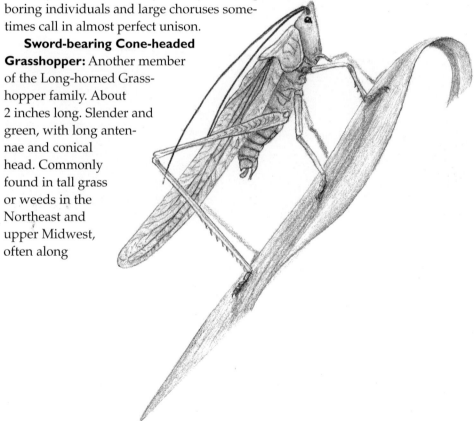

Sword-bearing Cone-headed Grasshopper

Northern True Katydid

roads and highways. Song is composed of very high-pitched, lispy notes given in rapid succession.

Pine Sawyer: Member of Cerambycidae, the Long-horned Beetle family. Adults about 1 inch long, elongated, with long antennae. Larvae of certain species, such as *Monochamus notatus*, the Northeastern Sawyer, bore into the trunks of dead or dying pines to feed on the inner bark, hence the name "Pine Sawyer." Larvae are white grubs with dark mouthparts; they grow to about 1 3/4 inch long. Pine Sawyer larvae make scraping and chewing noises when feeding. These sounds can be heard over 100 feet away on a quiet night.

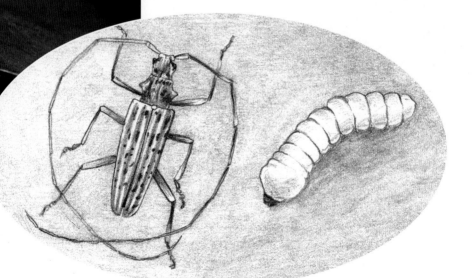

Wood-boring Pine-Sawyer larva and adult Long-horned Beetle

Raccoon

M ammals are distinguished by their covering of hair or fur as well as the mammary glands that nourish their young. Over 350 species inhabit North America. Most are nocturnal, secretive, and silent. However, a small number of species regularly produce loud and obvious night sounds that are among the most fascinating and human-like of all animal sounds.

Coyote: A grayish, doglike mammal with erect, pointed ears and a drooping tail carried low when running. Up to 4 feet long; weighs 18 to 30 pounds, with some individuals up to 50 pounds. Timid and wary. Inhabits

Coyote

American Beaver

deserts, prairies, and open woodlands in the West, and brushy forest in the East. Hybridizes with dogs and wolves. Vocalizes at night and at dusk and dawn. Produces outbursts of high-pitched and vibrant yips, yaps, and yapping howls that often end with a shrill, broken scream.

Raccoon: Common and widespread. Recognized by black mask over its eyes and alternating rings of yellow and black on its bushy tail. About 24 inches long; weighs up to 35 pounds. Chiefly nocturnal in habits. Dens in hollow trees, sometimes as a family group. In the wild, feeds mostly along the shorelines of streams and lakes. Also common in suburban areas where it raids trash cans for garbage. During fights, raccoons growl, bark, whine, and produce snarling screams that many people confuse with sounds made by quarreling housecats. Also make garbled, twittering sounds.

American Beaver: A widespread aquatic mammal with a broad, flat, hairless tail. About 28 inches long with 10-inch tail; adults weigh 30 to 60 pounds. Makes dams of sticks and mud and lives in conical houses made of

Porcupines

same. Chiefly nocturnal, but active at dusk and dawn. Feeds on the bark of living trees. Gnaws through limbs and trunks with huge front teeth and strips away the bark. An alarmed beaver slaps its tail against the water and then dives. The loud gnawing sounds of a feeding beaver can be heard several hundred feet away on a quiet night. Young make plaintive moaning sounds, usually from inside the den.

Porcupine: Heavy-bodied and clumsy-looking, with a lumbering walk. Recognized by sharp spines or quills emerging from fur on head, back, and tail. Up to 2 feet long with 10-inch tail; weighs 10 to 25 pounds. Prefers coniferous and mixed woods that grow in the West and Northeast and throughout Canada. Strips bark off trees and also eats buds, roots, and so forth. Readily climbs trees; primarily nocturnal in habits. Porcupines are seldom heard, but make a variety of grunts, groans, and cries, especially during the fall breeding season. Expressive, whining squeals are made by agitated porcupines during aggressive encounters.

River Otter

River Otter: A sleek, streamlined mammal with webbed toes and a heavy, rounded tail tapering to a point; excellent swimmer. Dark brown above, pale below. Over 2 feet long, with 15-inch tail. Associated with rivers, lakes, and streams, where it feeds on fish, frogs, crayfish, and so on. Principally nocturnal in habits. Gregarious and playful; often travels in family groups. Otters are usually silent, but they do make a variety of chirps, grunts, barks, and low growls. A prominent sound is a loud snort, given upon surfacing and periodically when feeding.

White-tailed Deer: The most widespread and familiar deer of North America. Adults about 6 feet long, with weights of 100 to 300 pounds or more (males are larger than females). Males grow and shed antlers annually. Prefers woodland edge habitats and thrives in agricultural areas with abundant forest cover. Most active at dusk and dawn. Whitetails are usually silent, but alarmed individuals respond with loud, airy snorts, sometimes accompanied by foot-stomping: *WHIEW!* They may then bound away excitedly with white-bottomed tail held erect.

White-tailed Deer

15. Loons

Common Loon

The loons are duck-like diving birds with webbed feet and long, pointed bills. Four species inhabit North America. All breed in the northern tundra regions; only the Common Loon breeds as far south as the United States. Loons are proficient divers, swimming to depths of 200 feet or more to capture fish, crustaceans, and other small aquatic animals. Loons take flight with difficulty, running along the surface of the water for a considerable distance before becoming airborne. All species are vocal on the breeding grounds where they utter wailing cries at night and sometimes a wild, demoniacal laughter that has given rise to the expression "crazy as a loon."

Common Loon: Breeds as far south as extreme northern United States; requires abundance of large lakes and ponds. About 32 inches long. Breeding birds have black head and bill, white necklace around black throat, and black back checkered with white. Wintering loons are pale gray. Common loons are highly vocal during the breeding season. When alarmed, they produce wavering, laugh-like "tremolo" calls. Members of a pair may alternate and overlap tremolo calls to produce a "tremolo duet." Another common call is a two- or three-parted "wail" reminiscent of the howling of a wolf. Wails help members of a pair maintain contact. Early in the breeding season, males produce loud, complex "yodel" calls that begin like the wail call, but end with ecstatic, undulating notes.

Master List of CD Contents

Group numbers are equivalent to the track numbers on the compact disc.

1. Thrushes
- Wood Thrush
- Veery
- Hermit Thrush
- Swainson's Thrush

2. Nightjars
- Whip-poor-will
- Chuck-will's-widow
- Common Poorwill
- Common Nighthawk

3. Shorebirds
- American Woodcock
- Common Snipe
- Killdeer
- Black-necked Stilt

4. Ducks and Geese
- Mallard
- Canada Goose

5. Owls
- Barred Owl
- Great Horned Owl
- Eastern Screech-Owl
- Western Screech-Owl
- Barn Owl
- Northern Saw-whet Owl

6. Frogs and Toads
- Spring Peeper
- Pacific Treefrog
- Pickerel Frog
- Western Chorus Frog
- Northern Cricket Frog
- Green Frog
- Bullfrog
- Pig Frog
- American Toad
- Fowler's Toad and
  Woodhouse's Toad

7. Rails and Relatives
- Clapper Rail
- Black Rail
- Sora
- Virginia Rail
- Yellow Rail
- Common Moorhen
- Sandhill Crane
- Limpkin

8. Alligators and Crocodiles
- American Alligator

9. Herons
- Great Blue Heron
- Black-crowned Night-Heron
- American Bittern

10. Wrens
Marsh Wren
Sedge Wren

11. Sparrows
White-throated Sparrow

12. Mimic Thrushes
Gray Catbird

13. Insects
Snowy Tree Cricket
Northern Mole Cricket
Carolina Ground Cricket
Northern True Katydid
Sword-bearing Cone-headed
Grasshopper
Pine Sawyer

14. Mammals
Coyote
Raccoon
American Beaver
Porcupine
River Otter
White-tailed Deer

15. Loons
Common Loon

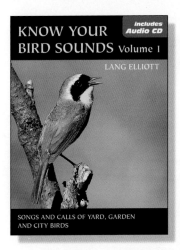
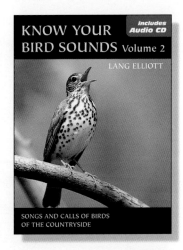

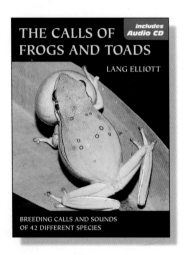